THIS BOOK BELONGS TO

_____

FOR THE KIDS WHO WANT TO WIN

ISBN: 9798894582153

ORION WAS THE YOUNGEST SPACE RANGER ON PLANET ZINDAR. ONE DAY, THE SKY TURNED DARK, AND THE PLANTS BEGAN TO WITHER. ZINDAR WAS IN TROUBLE.

THE WISE ELDER, SELAR, TOLD ORION ABOUT THE STAR CRYSTAL. "IT HOLDS THE POWER TO SAVE OUR PLANET," SELAR EXPLAINED. "BUT IT'S HIDDEN IN THE NEBULA MAZE."

RION PREPARED HIS STARSHIP, THE NOVA GLIDER. HE PACKED A MAP, FOOD CAPSULES, AND HIS TRUSTY ROBOT COMPANION, ZEBO. "LET'S SAVE ZINDAR," HE SAID.

THE NOVA GLIDER SOARED PAST GLITTERING STARS AND SWIRLING GALAXIES.
ZEBO BEEPED EXCITEDLY, "DESTINATION: NEBULA MAZE. DANGER LEVEL: HIGH!"

AS THEY NEARED THE NEBULA MAZE, COLORFUL CLOUDS SWIRLED LIKE A
GIANT PUZZLE. ORION TOOK A DEEP BREATH AND STEERED INTO THE MAZE.

INSIDE THE MAZE, ORION FOUND GLOWING PATHS THAT TWISTED AND TURNED.
"FOLLOW THE BRIGHTEST TRAIL," ZEBO SUGGESTED. ORION NODDED
AND NAVIGATED CAREFULLY.

SUDDENLY, A SWARM OF STAR SPRITES APPEARED. THE TINY, GLOWING
CREATURES CHIRPED, "SOLVE OUR RIDDLE TO PASS!"

THE STAR SPRITES ASKED, "WHAT HAS NO BEGINNING, NO END, AND BINDS THE GALAXY TOGETHER?" ORION THOUGHT HARD. "A CIRCLE!" HE ANSWERED.

THE STAR SPRITES CHEERED. "CORRECT! YOU MAY PASS." THEY
LIT THE PATH AHEAD, GUIDING ORION DEEPER INTO THE MAZE.

THE NEXT CHALLENGE WAS A RIVER OF SPARKLING STARDUST.
A BRIDGE FLOATED ABOVE IT, BUT IT WAS MISSING PIECES.

ZEBO SCANNED THE AREA. "BRIDGE PIECES ARE HIDDEN NEARBY." ORION
SEARCHED AND FOUND THEM, FITTING EACH PIECE CAREFULLY INTO PLACE.

WITH THE BRIDGE COMPLETE, ORION CROSSED SAFELY. THE RIVER
SHIMMERED BELOW, REFLECTING THE GLOW OF DISTANT STARS.

BEYOND THE RIVER, A FRIENDLY ALIEN NAMED LUMA APPEARED.
"I'LL HELP YOU IF YOU HELP ME," SHE SAID. HER SPACESHIP WAS STUCK.

ORION AND ZEBO WORKED TOGETHER TO FIX LUMA'S SHIP. "THANK YOU!" LUMA SAID.
"TAKE THIS CRYSTAL SHARD. IT WILL GUIDE YOU."

HE SHARD GLOWED AND POINTED THE WAY FORWARD. ORION THANKED
LUMA AND CONTINUED HIS JOURNEY, FEELING HOPEFUL.

SUDDENLY, A DARK SHADOW LOOMED OVERHEAD. IT WAS A SPACE BEAST WITH GLOWING RED EYES, BLOCKING THEIR PATH.

THE BEAST ROARED, "ONLY THOSE WHO ARE KIND MAY PASS."
ORION REMEMBERED THE FOOD CAPSULES IN HIS PACK.

HE OFFERED THE BEAST A CAPSULE. "HERE'S SOMETHING TO EAT."
THE BEAST SNIFFED, THEN SMILED. "YOU MAY PASS, KIND RANGER."

BEYOND THE BEAST, ORION FOUND A GLOWING DOORWAY. SYMBOLS COVERED ITS SURFACE. "IT'S A PUZZLE!" ZEBO EXCLAIMED.

ORION MATCHED THE SYMBOLS TO FORM A STAR PATTERN.
THE DOORWAY OPENED, REVEALING A SHIMMERING CAVERN.

INSIDE THE CAVERN, THE STAR CRYSTAL FLOATED, SURROUNDED BY LIGHT.
ORION APPROACHED CAREFULLY, HIS HEART POUNDING.

SUDDENLY, A VOICE ECHOED. "PROVE YOU ARE WORTHY OF THE STAR CRYSTAL,
" IT SAID. ORION STOOD TALL. "I SEEK IT TO SAVE MY PLANET."

THE VOICE REPLIED, "SHOW COURAGE, KINDNESS, AND WISDOM, AND THE CRYSTAL IS YOURS." ORION'S JOURNEY HAD PROVEN ALL THREE.

THE STAR CRYSTAL GLOWED BRIGHTER. IT FLOATED INTO ORION'S HANDS.
"YOU HAVE EARNED IT," THE VOICE SAID. "USE IT WISELY."

ORION AND ZEBO HURRIED BACK TO THE NOVA GLIDER. THE MAZE SEEMED
TO GUIDE THEM OUT, AS IF THE CRYSTAL'S MAGIC WAS HELPING.

AS THEY LEFT THE NEBULA MAZE, ORION SAW LUMA WAVING FROM HER SHIP.
"GOOD LUCK, SPACE RANGER!" SHE CALLED.

THE JOURNEY HOME WAS SMOOTH, THE CRYSTAL'S LIGHT LEADING
THE WAY. ORION COULDN'T WAIT TO SAVE ZINDAR.

WHEN THEY LANDED ON ZINDAR, THE PLANET LOOKED WORSE.
"WE'RE JUST IN TIME," ORION SAID, HURRYING TO THE ELDER.

SELAR GUIDED ORION TO THE PLANET'S CORE. "PLACE THE CRYSTAL
HERE," SHE SAID. ORION CAREFULLY SET IT IN PLACE.

THE CRYSTAL'S LIGHT SPREAD THROUGH ZINDAR, TURNING THE DARK
SKY BRIGHT AND BRINGING LIFE BACK TO THE PLANTS.

THE PEOPLE OF ZINDAR CHEERED. "ORION SAVED US!" THEY CRIED.
ORION FELT PROUD BUT HUMBLE. "WE DID IT TOGETHER," HE SAID.

ZEBO BEEPED HAPPILY. "MISSION ACCOMPLISHED!" ORION LAUGHED.
"WE MAKE A GREAT TEAM, ZEBO."

SELAR PRESENTED ORION WITH A MEDAL. "YOU ARE ZINDAR'S HERO,
" SHE SAID. "THE YOUNGEST AND BRAVEST SPACE RANGER."

THE PLANET BLOOMED WITH COLOR. ORION KNEW THE STAR CRYSTAL'S POWER HAD SAVED ZINDAR AND WOULD PROTECT IT FOR GENERATIONS.

AS THE STARS TWINKLED ABOVE, ORION LOOKED TO THE SKY.
"THE GALAXY IS FULL OF ADVENTURES," HE SAID. "AND I'M READY."

BACK AT THE NOVA GLIDER, ZEBO CHIRPED, "WHERE TO NEXT?"
ORION SMILED. "ANYWHERE THE STARS TAKE US."

THE NOVA GLIDER SOARED INTO SPACE, LEAVING A TRAIL OF LIGHT. ORION'S HEART SWELLED WITH EXCITEMENT FOR THE ADVENTURES AHEAD.

IN THE QUIET OF SPACE, ORION THOUGHT OF THE LESSONS HE HAD LEARNED: COURAGE, KINDNESS, AND WISDOM COULD OVERCOME ANY CHALLENGE.

THE STARS SEEMED TO WINK AT ORION AS HE WHISPERED, "THANK YOU, STAR CRYSTAL." THE GALAXY FELT LIKE HOME.

AND SO, THE YOUNGEST SPACE RANGER CONTINUED HIS JOURNEY, READY TO BRING HOPE AND LIGHT WHEREVER IT WAS NEEDED. THE END.